Multimedia Projects
in the Classroom

Multimedia Projects in the Classroom

A Guide to Development and Evaluation

Timothy D. Green
Abbie Brown

CORWIN PRESS, INC.
A Sage Publications Company
Thousand Oaks, California

For information:

Corwin Press, Inc.
A Sage Publications Company
2455 Teller Road
Thousand Oaks, California 91320
E-mail: order@corwinpress.com

Sage Publications Ltd.
6 Bonhill Street
London EC2A 4PU
United Kingdom

Sage Publications India Pvt. Ltd.
M-32 Market
Greater Kailash I
New Delhi 110 048 India

Printed in the United States of America

Library of Congress Cataloging-in-Publication Data

Green, Timothy D., 1968-
    Multimedia projects in the classroom: A guide to development and evaluation / by Timothy D. Green and Abbie Brown.
        p. cm.
    Includes bibliographical references and index.
    ISBN 0-7619-7852-6 (c) — ISBN 0-7619-7853-4 (p)
    1. Media programs (Education) 2. Curriculum planning. 3. Educational technology.   I. Title: Multimedia projects in the classroom. II. Brown, Abbie. III. Title.
    LB1028.4 .G76 2002
    371.33'467—dc21   2001005328

This book is printed on acid-free paper.

01 02 03 04 05 10 9 8 7 6 5 4 3 2 1

Acquisitions Editor:	Robb Clouse
Associate Editor:	Kylee Liegl
Editorial Assistant:	Erin Buchanan
Production Editor:	Diane S. Foster
Copy Editor:	Marilyn P. Scott
Typesetter/Designer:	Denyse Dunn/Larry K. Bramble
Indexer:	Molly Hall
Cover Designer:	Michael Dubowe

Contents

··

Preface

··

Teachers have been working with multimedia for a very long time. Slide shows, recordings, even drawing on the chalkboard mixed with written words—all of these make use of multiple media. However, since powerful personal computers became part of the classroom in the late 1980s and early 1990s, multimedia projects have taken on a new and very different look and feel, something that is both wonderfully exciting and a little scary. We know firsthand: We were classroom teachers during that time.

As more powerful computers with multimedia capabilities become available in classrooms and teachers become increasingly pressured to integrate technology into their curriculums, an up-to-date "how-to" book on classroom multimedia development is necessary and important. This book's goal is to help teachers understand the multimedia development process so that they may incorporate student-produced multimedia projects into their curriculums.

This book is grouped into five chapters. The first four chapters address issues of integrating multimedia production into the classroom, beginning with "Why Are We Doing This?" in Chapter 1. We discuss issues of curriculum integration, planning, and classroom management in Chapters 2 and 3, and focus on evaluation of student work in Chapter 4. Chapter 5 explains how professional multimedia producers work and includes some of the more common jargon and procedures used in the industry.

It is our hope that teachers everywhere will feel the same excitement and satisfaction that we have in facilitating student-made, digital, multimedia projects as part of their curriculums and that this book will help in this endeavor.

Acknowledgments

The authors would like to thank the following people for their generous contributions of time, expertise, and artifacts that helped shape this book:

- Rob McPherson and Julie Lippay and the members of the afterschool video club at Franklin Elementary School in Pullman, Washington, for sharing their scripts and storyboards.
- Christine Olmstead and her sixth-grade students at the Mariposa Elementary School in Brea, California, for sharing their storyboards and PowerPoint projects.
- Bob Appelman and Elizabeth Boling at Indiana University's Department of Instructional Systems Technology for sharing their grading rubric for instructional media projects.

Special thanks go to Robb Clouse, Acquisitions Editor at Corwin Press, for taking a chance on new authors and supporting the idea for this book.

The contributions of the following reviewers are also gratefully acknowledged.

Bridget Weishaar
Technology Instructor
The Latin School of Chicago
Chicago, IL

Connie Louie
Technology Director
Massachusetts Department of Education
Malden, MA

Maria J. Vlahos
Mathematics Department Chair
Loyola Academy
Wilmette, IL

About the Authors

Abbie Brown holds a PhD in Instructional Systems Technology from Indiana University and an MA from Teachers College at Columbia University. He is currently a professor of Educational Technology and Instructional Design at Washington State University. Previously, he taught at the Bank Street School for Children in New York City and George Washington Middle School in New Jersey. He has received awards for outstanding teaching and curriculum design from the New Jersey Department of Education and is an experienced instructional media producer and interface designer.

Timothy D. Green holds a PhD in Instructional Systems Technology and Curriculum and Instruction from Indiana University. He has taught grades K-12. His expertise is in multimedia design and the integration of technology into the teaching and learning process. He is currently a professor of elementary education at California State University, Fullerton.

*We would like to dedicate this book to all the teachers
we have worked with as students, colleagues,
and mentors, who have shaped our thinking
about multimedia in the classroom
. . . and, of course, our moms.*

CHAPTER 1

What Is Multimedia?

Chapter Guiding Questions

This chapter will help you answer the following questions:

- What is the formal definition of the term *multimedia?*
- Is it appropriate to integrate multimedia production projects into K-12 classroom activity?
- What are the basic elements of multimedia?
- What is the difference between analog and digital media?

Digital Multimedia in the Classroom

Students of almost any age are capable of creating digital multimedia projects. The hardware and software have become relatively inexpensive, and, for better or worse (mostly better, we would argue) there has been a concerted effort made to get computing tools into K-12 classrooms.

Why Are We Doing This? The Importance of Integrating Digital Media Into the Classroom

Considerable debate has arisen about how, when, or even if computers and computing tools should be integrated into the school day, but the fact remains that vast numbers of teachers are faced with the responsibility of finding meaningful activities that incorporate computers into their classrooms. The publication of the International Society for Technology in Education's (ISTE, 2000) *National Educational Technology Standards for Students* and the adoption of these standards by a wide variety of educational organizations give teachers, parents, and administrators some direction in this area. When teachers provide opportunities for students to work on digital multimedia projects, they are addressing at least three of ISTE's technology foundation standards for students:

- Students use technology tools to enhance learning, increase productivity, and promote creativity.
- Students use productivity tools to collaborate in constructing technology-enhanced models, prepare publications, and produce other creative works.
- Students use a variety of media and formats to communicate information and ideas effectively to multiple audiences.

Currently, there is a great deal of discussion among educators about the concepts of visual literacy and media literacy, particularly as they relate to digital multimedia. These terms are often used to refer to students developing sophistication in interpreting complex messages sent via educational software, video games, digital video, broadcast television, and Web sites. Student-produced multimedia projects can help develop visual and media literacy skills by providing students with opportunities to examine the component parts of multimedia and the ways in which each of the parts are used to create elaborate and evocative presentations.

Perhaps one of the most compelling reasons for incorporating multimedia production projects into any classroom is the excitement these projects tend to generate among students. Making presentations that make noise, move, and offer surprises to the user are a great deal of fun for everyone. As classroom teachers and college-level educational technology instructors, we can say from experience that students seem to find digital multimedia production projects deeply satisfying, and they enjoy sharing these projects with peers, other teachers, and parents.

Multimedia Defined

The term *multimedia* has been part of our language since the 1950s. It has been used to refer to a great many aspects of communication and technology and is therefore difficult to precisely define.

- According to Tay Vaughan (1994), author of *Multimedia: Making it Work,* multimedia is "any combination of text, graphic art, sound, animation, and video delivered to you by computer or other electronic means" (p. 4).
- According to Roy Rada (1995), author of *Interactive Media,* the term refers to any *synchronized* media streams. One example is that of moving images synchronized with sound (such as a television broadcast or a modern film).
- According to Heinich, Molenda, Russell, and Smaldino (1999), the authors of *Instructional Media and Technologies for Learning,* the term "refers to any combination of two or more media formats that are integrated to form an informational or instructional program" (p. 229).

Basically, *multimedia* is used any time one medium of communication is coordinated with another medium to transmit information in some unified manner. Multimedia may be thought of as any method of transmitting information using at least two of the following: graphics; audio, text, and interactivity (often, this refers to the navigational components of a computer program).

Multimedia must first be designed and produced, then stored or saved for use at a later time. The most common methods of storing multimedia information currently include paper, slides, transparency, audiotape, videotape, film, and digital storage devices, such as a computer hard drive, floppy disk, CD (compact disc), and CD-ROM (compact disc, read-only memory). The most common methods of presenting multimedia may combine any of the following:

- Paper-based—books, magazines, brochures
- Light-based—slide shows, overhead transparency presentations
- Audio-based—record players, CD players, cassette tape players, radio
- Moving-image-based—television broadcasts, VCR (video cassette recorder), film
- Digitally based—computer (via input and output devices, most commonly a monitor, audio speakers, keyboard, and mouse)

The Difference Between Multimedia and Media

Any one of the types of communication, production, storage, or presentation items listed earlier may be accurately referred to singly as a medium; two or more of these items are referred to as *media*. Multimedia, in the strictest sense, refers to some combination of two or more methods of conveying information. The distinction between media and multimedia is blurred by the fact that the terms can refer to the type of information, the type of storage, or the method of transmission. The distinction is further blurred by the capacities of the various transmission methods (e.g., is videotape a single medium or is it multimedia because it can store images and sound? [Brown, 1999, pp. 16-17]). We use the term *multimedia* to refer to a deliberate attempt to convey graphical (images and text) and/or auditory information through any of the aforementioned methods of storage or transmission.

For this book's purposes, it is probably easiest to think of multimedia as the general term that includes these three common classroom activities: video production (making something that is presented on videotape), desktop publishing (making a product that is presented on paper), and programming for interactivity (making a product that is presented on a computer). See Figure 1.1 for the differences between multimedia, hypertext, and hypermedia.

More Information About Specific Media Types

Graphics

A graphic is something we perceive through a visually-based medium. Any two-dimensional images are considered graphics. Even if the image is rendered in "3-D," it is still presented via a two-dimensional medium, such as paper or a television

---

Figure 1.1. Multimedia, Hypertext, and Hypermedia: What's the Difference?

Multimedia, hypertext, and hypermedia are terms that get thrown around a great deal, both by the truly geeky and by those who aspire to geekiness. Just to set the record straight, this is a (somewhat oversimplified) breakdown of what these terms mean and how they relate to each other:

- *Multimedia* is the use of two or more media to present information.
- *Hypertext* is a nonlinear method of presenting text. Examples of this include Web pages that have words or phrases that, when clicked on, take the reader to another section of the Web and "choose your own adventure" books that ask the reader to make a choice as he or she reads and, based on the choices made, direct the reader to specific pages later in the book.
- *Hypermedia* is the multimedia version of hypertext. Hypermedia uses a variety of media that are linked in a manner that allows the user to go to various other media in a nonlinear fashion (the World Wide Web can be considered an example of hypermedia).

---

monitor. These images may be either attempts at a true representation of reality, such as photographs, or iconic representations of reality. One example of an iconic representation is the pair of graphics typically displayed on restroom doors to indicate whether they are men's rooms or women's rooms (see Figure 1.2).

Graphics can be either still images or moving images. Still image graphics include photographs, digital images, paintings, and posters. Still images are measured by both size (sometimes called the canvas size) and resolution, that is "dots per inch" on paper, or "pixels per inch" on a computer screen.

Moving-image graphics include photographic types of images that, when shown in rapid succession, give the illusion of seeing real places and animated types of images, which in turn give the impression of cartoonlike drawings moving. Video, film, and computer environments provide storage and presentation methods for moving images. Moving images are measured in terms of projection size, resolution, and duration.

Audio

Audio is any sound-based medium; anything we hear or listen to. Sound is transmitted through waves (that's why no one can hear you scream in space and why rocket scientists find it vexing that science fiction programs often have sounds accompanying explosions that occur in space—in a vacuum, there is no way for waves to form). When dealing with audio, we tend to measure it in terms of loudness (amplitude) and duration.

Figure 1.2. Iconic Graphics Traditionally Used to Depict Gender-Specific Facilities

Text

Text is a visual medium composed entirely of symbols that are used to represent spoken language. Text may vary in terms of the typeface (or font) used and its size (this font, for example, is ZapfEllipt BT; its size is 11 point).Text is measured in terms of length (usually, the number of words or pages) and size (the picas or point size: Standard text is 10 or 12 points; the larger the number, the bigger the text).

Interactivity

Interactivity is not exactly a medium; it is the design idea behind a multimedia project. Interactivity allows a person to access the various media included in the project in a meaningful way. Interactivity can also be referred to as *interface design* or *human factors design*. The interactivity or interface design is the framework that the multimedia producer creates to make the product both a useful and satisfying experience for the user.

Interactivity takes into account the choice of a strategy for organizing information. According to Wurman and Bradford (1997), authors of *Information Architects,* there are only five ways that information can be organized: by location, alphabetically, chronologically (a timeline), categorically, or by hierarchy.

There are essentially two possible interface structures for any multimedia project:

- A linear structure, which provides the user with a directed or single-choice situation (see Figure 1.3)

- A nonlinear structure, which provides the user with a decision-based or multiple-choice design (see Figure 1.4)

At the design stage of a multimedia project, interactivity is measured by the amount of control the designer wants the user to have over the sequence and pace

Figure 1.3. This HyperStudio Card Makes Use of a Linear Navigation Strategy

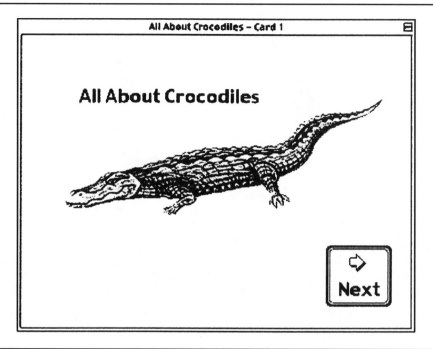

of the presentation. After the multimedia project is produced, interactivity is measured by the perceived usability of the project by the intended user. Usability testing is an art unto itself, requiring careful planning and some understanding of how research is conducted (suggestions for conducting a simple usability test are given later in this book).

Digital Media

Digital media are any media that have been translated into a format that can be interpreted, stored, and displayed by a computer. Computers process information in a binary format (at the most elemental level, all computing activity can be reduced to a series of ones and zeroes). Therefore, any medium processed through a computer must be translated to a binary format. Graphics must be translated into a series of ones and zeroes that the computer can interpret. Audio sounds must be translated into a series of ones and zeroes that the computer can interpret. Actions that can occur and navigation choices the user makes (the interactivity) must be translated into a series of ones and zeroes.

Digital media are different from analog media. Analog media includes videotape, audiotape, and painting with canvas and oils (to name just a few—there are hundreds of analog media). The largest difference between analog and digital media is that analog media may not be compatible with other analog media (you cannot store an oil painting on a piece of audiotape), whereas all digital media are essen-

Figure 1.4. This HyperStudio Card Makes Use of a Nonlinear Navigation Strategy

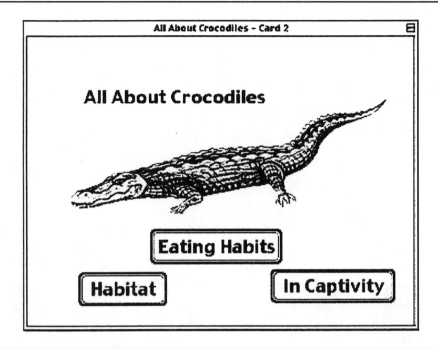

tially compatible because they are all stored in the same format (a series of ones and zeroes). Figure 1.5 reiterates the differences between digital and analog.

Types of Digital Multimedia

For purposes of working with digital multimedia in the classroom, it is necessary to consider two specific types of digital multimedia: networked and single computer.

Networked and Single Computer

Networked multimedia allow the user to make use of media that are shared by a number of computers connected together. The Internet is such a network (it is the biggest one, encompassing the entire world). Single-computer multimedia presume that the computer the user has access to is not connected to any other computers and that all the media needed by the user reside within that one computer's storage area(s).

Networked multimedia are a distributed resource; the information stored on any one computer is available to a number of other computers. Typically, this is accomplished through a server-client relationship. A *server* is any computer dedicated to the task of storing information that can be retrieved by another computer. A *client* is any computer that requests information from a server. For example, when you use your home computer to shop for a book online, your computer becomes the client requesting information from a server: Your computer is the client computer

---

Figure 1.5. The Difference Between Digital and Analog

Digital refers to a method of representing information as a series of bits that represent on or off states (ones and zeroes). This is a binary method of expressing information because there are only two possibilities for any discrete piece of information.

Analog refers to a method of representing information as a series of continuously varying physical quantities. The classic example of an analog representation is the use of a clock with a face and hands that continuously change to indicate the current time.

---

receiving media from "bookstogo.com," which is the server computer sending media to your computer. The World Wide Web is an example of networked multimedia. Using a browser (the most common are Netscape Navigator and Internet Explorer), one can access a Web site that is stored on a server in Australia; that Web site may make use of video clips that are stored on a server in Canada and graphic images that are stored on a server in Germany. The client computer receives all of the information from the World Wide Web and presents it to the user. Creating Web pages is currently the most common form of networked multimedia production. Networked multimedia projects are often stored on remote servers (although they can easily be stored on a local computer if they are not for public display); many school districts now operate their own servers and set aside some portion of the storage space for class projects.

Single-computer multimedia are a self-contained resource. All available media are stored nearby in the computer's own storage system or are directly connected to that one computer (one example of nearby storage is laser disc players that are controlled by a computer). The single-computer model assumes that the computer in use has no connection (is not networked) to other computers. Common forms of classroom-based single-computer multimedia production include presentations made with Microsoft's PowerPoint software and projects created using HyperStudio software. Single-computer multimedia projects are often stored by creating a CD-ROM of the project. A CD-ROM creation device is called a *burning unit* because it uses a small laser to etch binary code into the plastic CD; a variety of these units are easy to use and available at relatively modest prices—the CDs themselves are available in bulk for well under a dollar apiece.

Summary

Multimedia are created any time one medium of communication is coordinated with another medium to transmit information in some unified manner. The major components of multimedia projects are graphics, audio, text, and interactivity. *Multimedia* may refer to production, storage, or presentation technologies. *Digital multimedia* refer to any combination of media that can be interpreted, stored, and displayed by a computer. The two types of digital multimedia presentations are networked and single computer.

Many teachers are receiving pressure of various kinds to incorporate computers and computing activities into the classroom. A recent and well-received initiative by ISTE to develop a set of standards for educational technology recommends using computing tools to promote creativity, productivity, and effective communication skills. Digital multimedia production projects in the classroom can be fun and satisfying experiences. These types of activities are also generally supported by educators interested in fostering visual and media literacy.

Frequently Asked Questions About Multimedia

Question: Are multimedia production tools easy to use?

Answer: It depends on the tool. Some, like tape recorders, are so common to most people that they can be picked up and used immediately. Some, like video editing equipment or authoring software, require practice. It is always a good idea to assume that it will take an investment of at least a few hours alone to practice with a new production tool.

Question: Is it easy to teach students how to use multimedia production tools?

Answer: The majority of students are eager to learn how to use these tools, which makes teaching their use a bit easier. We have generally found that the more comfortable the teacher is with the tool, the easier it is for them to teach its use. The most effective approach we have seen is that of the teacher as a fellow learner—the teacher takes the approach of knowing just a little bit more than the student, with everyone learning more about how the tool works. Once students understand the basics of a multimedia production tool, they are often able to teach their peers how to use it, and every individual will find something new to share with the group.

Question: Are digital media production tools expensive?

Answer: Yes, digital media production tools, hardware and software, are expensive. However, they are getting less so every month (a good digital camera is now available for a fraction of its price two years ago). Hardware and software is often available for teachers and schools at a significant discount (referred to as *education pricing),* and many of the more expensive software tools have so-called academic versions (versions with a bit less power than the professional versions) that sell for a fraction of the professional version cost.

References

Brown, A. H. (1999). *Strategies for the delivery of instructional design coursework: Helping learners develop a professional attitude toward the production process* (UMI Publication Number AAT 9962697). Doctoral dissertation, Indiana University, Bloomington.

Heinich, R., Molenda, M., Russell, J., & Smaldino, S. (1999). *Instructional media and technologies for learning* (6th ed.). NJ: Merrill/Prentice Hall.

International Society for Technology in Education. (2000). *National educational technology standards for students.* Eugene, OR: Author.

Rada, R. (1995). *Interactive media.* New York: Springer-Verlag.

Vaughan, T. (1994). *Multimedia: Making it work* (2nd ed.). New York: McGraw-Hill.

Wurman, R. S., & Bradford, P. (1997). *Information architects.* New York: Graphis.

Recommended Reading

Brunner, C., & Tally, W. (1999). *The new media literacy handbook.* New York: Anchor.

Kristof, R., & Satran, A. (1995). *Interactivity by design: Creating and communicating with new media.* Mountain View, CA: Adobe.

Schneiderman, B. (1998). *Designing the user interface: Strategies for effective human-computer interaction* (3rd ed.). Reading, MA: Addison-Wesley.

Integrating Curriculum Content Into Multimedia Production

Chapter Guiding Questions

This chapter will help you answer the following questions:

- What are recommended approaches to integrating curriculum content into multimedia production projects?

- What are some traditional classroom multimedia activities?

- Where can I find resources that address the issue of technology-curriculum integration?

According to the ISTE's (2000) *National Educational Technology Standards for Students*, "Curriculum integration with the use of technology involves the infusion of technology as a tool to enhance the learning in a content area or multidisciplinary setting" (p. 6). This is an important thing to remember . . . and unfortunately all too often overlooked: Working with multimedia production in the classroom should be an activity that primarily enhances traditional content learning.

As we have mentioned before, multimedia production can be an exciting and highly satisfying activity. Working on multimedia production addresses the need for students to increase their ability to create and communicate, improving their media literacy skills as well as fostering their capabilities with computing technologies. It is important to keep in mind that developing multimedia production and media literacy skills does not need to occur in a "content vacuum." Curriculum content that would or should be covered in the course of the school year can be an integral part of a multimedia production project.

A Brief History of Multimedia in the Classroom

Teachers have been incorporating multimedia projects in their classrooms for years. It may come as a surprise that the first use of multimedia in the classroom actually had nothing to do with a computer! Teachers had been using and teaching their students how to develop and use multimedia projects long before computers became commonplace in classrooms. School plays, school newspapers, and yearbooks are all examples of multimedia projects that have been developed and used in the classroom without the use of computers.

The types of multimedia projects that teachers currently develop and use with their students have changed significantly in the past 20 years. The change has come about because of the development of the computer and its availability in the classroom. Despite the change, teachers and students still develop and use multimedia projects that do not rely on computers.

There are two general types of multimedia projects—the classical media production project and the digital multimedia project. The classical media production project is the precursor to what we now consider the digital multimedia project. The major difference between the two is that the classical media production project is in an analog format, not digital; in other words, the classical media production project is not computer based (see Chapter 1 for a description of the difference between analog and digital formats). The two project types do share a common component that all multimedia projects share: the use of a combination of at least two media elements (text, graphics, audio, and interactivity).

Multimedia in the Classroom

Multimedia projects range from the very basic to the complex. In a basic form, multimedia can be text and graphics on paper. In a more complex form, multimedia can be a computer simulation or game, where text, graphics, audio, and a high level of interactivity are combined together. We have said there are two types of multimedia projects—classical media production projects and digital media projects. A few selected multimedia projects of each type are described in the discussion that follows as examples of the kinds of projects that integrate multimedia production into the K-12 curriculum.

Classical Media Production Projects

The morning announcements. Almost every school has some form of announcements made over a schoolwide PA system. The announcements are typically given by students and describe important events related to the school. In middle schools, junior highs, and high schools, the announcements include information about sporting events, school plays, dances, club meetings, and so forth. In elementary grades, the announcements typically include the lunch menu, the Pledge of Allegiance, important reminders of upcoming events, poems written by students, and the "quote of the day" or other inspirational messages.

The morning announcement requires the combination of text, the spoken word, and other audio elements (i.e., music, sound effects). Students learn a great deal in the process of developing and delivering the morning announcements. Students, working with teachers, develop the text that will be read. This can include gathering information from students, teachers, the principal, secretaries, and other school personnel. The copy is organized, edited, and approved for reading over the PA system. Students reading the announcements practice the announcements prior to going "on air."

Closed-system school radio. Some middle schools, junior highs, and high schools allow music to be played over the school PA system during the school day (e.g., before morning classes, during lunch, and after school). The musical airwaves are staffed by "disc-jockey wannabes"—typically, two or three students who have expressed interest. Working with a teacher, the students are responsible for selecting a play list of songs; the teacher responsible for the students approves the songs that are appropriate to be played. The students may also be responsible for making announcements, introducing songs, making song dedications, and more. This project obviously includes both text and audio.

The school newspaper. The school newspaper is a more involved project than the morning announcements or the closed-system school radio. The school newspaper requires the work of several students with the assistance of a teacher or two. Students work in different roles, such as editor, assistant editor, reporters, and photographers. They are responsible for finding and writing stories, checking for accuracy of information, editing, taking pictures, and deciding on the layout of these elements before the newspaper is printed. Teachers working with the students guide them through the process. Text and graphics are important elements of the school newspaper project, and students learn a great deal about communicating in terms of both content and form.

Yearbooks. The school yearbook is a yearlong project that requires many of the same student and teacher roles as a school newspaper project. There is an editor, assistant editor, reporters or writers, and photographers. Students gather information (text and graphics), edit the information, and place the information into a suitable layout. The teacher in charge of the students guides the students as they make decisions on what to include in the yearbook and how it will look.

School plays. A school play is another major classical media project that includes text, graphics, and audio, making it very much a multimedia production. A teacher acts as the director, making sure the play is properly coordinated (often with the help of a student stage manager). Students take on a variety of roles—actors, set designers, costume designers, musicians, and lighting and sound technicians, to name a few. The combination and careful coordination of different media is crucial for the success of a school play.

Digital Multimedia Production Projects

There are numerous digital multimedia projects that can be developed and used in the classroom. Digital multimedia projects use a variety of software packages that allow teachers and students to manipulate text, graphics, and audio and to incorporate interactivity into a project. One such type of software commonly used to create digital multimedia projects is multimedia authoring software (see Figure 2.1 for some examples of multimedia authoring software). Several examples of digital multimedia projects are described in the sections to follow.

PowerPoint project. A common PowerPoint project is one designed to correspond with a speech or a presentation being given on a particular topic. A teacher or student can create a presentation—a series of individual slides with text, graphics, and even audio—that enhances the speech or presentation being made by allowing the audience to see examples of what is being reported on. For example, a student who has been assigned to give an oral presentation on leopards can create a PowerPoint project that can be used while the oral presentation is given. The PowerPoint presentation can textually outline important facts and information about leopards and show graphics depicting what leopards look like.

HyperStudio project. There are a variety of HyperStudio projects that teachers and students can develop and use. One example is a "Digital Me-Book" (this project is based on an activity from the book, *Tribes,* by Jeanne Gibbs, 1995). With the Digital Me-Books, students develop a HyperStudio stack that represents a "book" by creating cards that describe how they feel and things they like. For example, one card could read, "I feel good when I do well in school." The cards can also be illustrated; students can scan illustrations they have made or draw illustrations directly in HyperStudio.

Video school news production project. With airtime on public access television stations available to schools and closed-circuit school broadcast systems, schools have been taking advantage of the opportunity to be on television by creating and airing school news segments. Students take on a variety of roles in this project— director, producer, reporters, anchors, engineers, and camera-people. The final product that is created is a news program that has been edited on a computer video editing system. This project includes a heavy use of media.

Each teacher is going to know more about his or her specific curriculum than we could, and we would not presume to dictate curricular goals. However, we can articulate a few basics of instructional design and recommend a number of resources that may help form and strengthen the bridge between traditional curriculum content and the use of innovative media technologies.

Well-designed instruction should have carefully considered objectives and should involve students in activities that cause them to want to achieve those objectives. Learning objectives should be clearly articulated ahead of time, and methods of evaluating whether those objectives have been met should be part of the lesson plan. One way to be sure that traditional content (e.g., science, mathematics, writing)

Figure 2.1. Multimedia Authoring Software Examples

Multimedia authoring software allows a user to create a product that combines text, audio, video, and interactivity. A variety of companies create software that can be considered multimedia authoring software. Three examples follow:

The main differences between the software packages are (a) the functions available to the user, (b) the learning curve involved in knowing how to use the software, and (c) the price of the software. For example, Macromedia Director is professional-quality multimedia authoring software (some commercial-quality software games are created using Director). It has numerous functions and options, allowing a great amount of control in the type of product that can be created. However, it is difficult to learn (its learning curve is high), and it is relatively expensive.

Microsoft PowerPoint: PowerPoint is designed to work like a "digital overhead projector." It allows a user to create presentations that are made up of individual slides. Each slide corresponds approximately to the size of a computer screen. Each slide can include a variety of media. PowerPoint presentation interface structures are typically linear (see Chapter 1 for a description of interface structures).

HyperStudio (http://www.hyperstudio.com/): HyperStudio imitates index cards. The index cards (called cards) are combined to create a stack. A stack is a series of cards that can be navigated through via buttons a user creates. Each card can include a variety of media. Stack interface structures can be nonlinear or linear; typically they are nonlinear.

Macromedia Director (http://www.macromedia.com/): Director uses the metaphor of a play as its interface. Media elements (text, graphics, and audio) are called *cast members*. The combination of these elements into a product is called a movie. Most projects created using Director have a nonlinear interface structure.

is well integrated into the multimedia production activity is to incorporate content objectives into the lesson plan from the start.

It is relatively easy to create a set of instructional objectives that covers both technology standards and the standards set forth by organizations that address traditional content or local curricular directives. For example, the recommendation, "Students read a wide range of literature from many periods in many genres to build an understanding of the many dimensions (e.g., philosophical, ethical and aesthetic) of human experience," from the *Standards for the English Language Arts* of the International Reading Association and National Council of Teachers of English (1996), works well with the national educational technology standard, "Students use telecommunications to collaborate, publish, and interact with peers, experts, and other audiences" (ISTE, 2000, p. 4A). Applying both of these standards in such a way that students are given opportunities to read from a wide variety of literature, synthesize their reading, and develop a multimedia presentation of their synthesized thoughts to share with an audience should strengthen the learning experience.

A multimedia project should not be viewed as taking time away from more traditional curriculum content. It should be something that causes students to get excited about learning more about the traditional content and to apply the most basic skills of writing, reading, and calculating in a way that is immediately relevant. A multimedia production project may motivate students to become more involved with the content, assuming of course they want to work with the new media. It has been our experience as teachers that most students look at traditional content with "fresh eyes and ears" when innovative technologies become part of the presentation.

Books That Address Technology-Curriculum Integration

We recommend three publications, both for their own content as well as for the resources they list:

- *The National Educational Technology Standards for Students*, written and published by the International Society for Technology in Education (ISTE, 2000) is an excellent resource. We have referred to the ISTE standards a number of times in this book because they are both useful and widely accepted in the education community. Besides listing a set of technology standards, the book contains a number of sample lessons that incorporate technology into traditional curriculum. The book also has an invaluable appendix that concisely lists curriculum standards recommended by the U.S. national organizations that coordinate activities for English language arts, foreign language, information literacy, mathematics, science, and social studies.

- *The Digital Classroom: How Technology Is Changing the Way We Teach and Learn*, edited by David T. Gordon (2000). This book contains a number of highly informative essays on the subject of teaching and technology, specifically addressing the integration of science, math, history, and literacy as well as providing a number of very useful addresses to sites on the World Wide Web.

- *The New Media Literacy Handbook: An Educator's Guide to Bringing New Media Into the Classroom*, written by Cornelia Brunner and William Tally (1999). This too is an informative and useful book that is divided into chapters that address the integration of innovative technologies and social studies, arts education, language arts, and science.

Resources on the World Wide Web

A number of Web sites exist that facilitate the integration of innovative multimedia technologies and curriculum. The following are among the best:

Computer Technology and Teaching (Theory and Application) Sites

Apple Learning Interchange
http://ali.apple.com/

Center for Children and Technology
http://www2.edc.org/CCT/cctweb/

Education With New Technologies
http://learnweb.harvard.edu/ent/home/index.cfm

Focus on Technology. A Web page by the National Education Association (NEA)
http://www.nea.org/cet/index_educator.html

The U.S. Department of Education Office of Technology
http://www.ed.gov/Technology/

Media Resources

Absolutely Free Clip Art
http://www.allfree-clipart.com/

Classical MIDI Archives (Digitized Musical Selections)
http://www.prs.net/midi.html

Footage.net, The Stock, Archival and News Footage Network
http://www.footage.net/

The Library of Congress On-Line
http://marvel.loc.gov/homepage/lchp.html

NASA's public access site for earth and space data
http://observe.ivv.nasa.gov/

The Smithsonian Institution (Commercial publication or exploitation of Smithsonian files is specifically prohibited; however, files may be used for nonprofit purposes.)
http://www.si.edu/

Web Clip Art: a large archive of royalty-free images
http://www.webclipart.about.com/internet/webclipart/

Organizations That the Computing Teacher May Want to Know More About

American Association of Computing in Education (AACE)

Publishes a number of journals in educational technology, curriculum, and teacher education, including *Journal of Technology and Teacher Education* and *Educational Technology Review*
http://www.aace.org/

Association for Computing Machinery (ACM)

Publishes interactions and communications of the ACM
http://www.acm.org/

Association of Educational Communications and Technology (AECT)

Publishes *TechTrends, Educational Technology Research & Development*
http://www.aect.org/

The Intellectual Property Resource Center, Kansas State University
http://www.ksu.edu/uauc/intprop/production.htm

International Society for Technology in Education (ISTE)

Publishes *Learning and Leading with Technology, the Journal of Research on Computing in Education,* and organizes the National Educational Computing Conference (NECC)
http://www.iste.org/

Summary

Curriculum content and multimedia production projects are not mutually exclusive. Multimedia production projects may actually increase the students' attention toward and satisfaction with curriculum content by providing an exciting and challenging medium through which to experience the content.

Classical media production projects, such as the school newspaper and the school play, have long been an important part of school activity, offering students opportunities to learn important communication skills as well as reinforcing the content of the traditional curriculum.

A variety of print and Web-based resources exist to facilitate the incorporation of traditional content into multimedia production projects. In this chapter, we have offered recommendations for three texts that are particularly useful in this area as well as a variety of Web addresses (URLS) to sites that specialize in this type of activity.

Frequently Asked Questions About Integrating
Curriculum Content Into Multimedia Production

Question: How much does it cost to join organizations like ISTE and AACE?

Answer: Membership dues for organizations such as these range from approximately $40 to $90 annually. There are usually significant discounts for undergraduate and graduate students. Membership almost always comes with a free subscription to at least one of the organization's publications as well as discounts on other publications.

Question: How do the free, online media resources compare to media resource packages available for purchase?

Answer: There are a wide variety of media resources available free online and an equally wide variety of media resources available for sale (usually in the form of CD-ROM-based libraries of sounds, images, or video clips). The quality of these resources runs the complete range, and the adage "you get what you pay for" is not always true in this instance. If you are thinking of spending money on a media resource package, check to see if there is a reasonable return policy. Some software retailers do not accept opened software packages for refund.

Question: If I have never developed a digital multimedia project for classroom or personal use, where should I start?

Answer: It depends on the skills you have and your objective for creating the multimedia project. If your skills are low, we suggest that you practice using the digital multimedia tools that are described in this book before jumping into creating a multimedia project. (We also suggest you finish reading the entire book even before this, of course!) There are some things you should learn how to do: Learn how to digitize images and sounds. Learn how to use multimedia authoring software, too. Once you feel comfortable with these two areas of multimedia development, you can tackle the process of creating your own project and then teaching your students how to do the same!

Question: Are classical media production projects really considered multimedia projects?

Answer: Yes! The difference between the two types of projects is that classical media production projects historically did not use computer-based technologies. Keep in mind the definition of multimedia given in Chapter 1: "Multimedia may be thought of as any method of transmitting information using at least two of the following: graphics, audio, text, and interactivity (often this refers to the navigational components of a computer program)." Classical media production projects, such as a school newspaper, may only include graphics and text. Granted, this may not fit what most people think of when they hear the term *multimedia projects;* however, they are definitely multimedia projects.

Question: Where can I get additional ideas for multimedia projects I can have my students create?

Answer: There are a variety of books, journals, magazines, listservs, Web sites, and organizations that can provide ideas on multimedia projects that you can use with your students. Chapter 6 lists a variety of resources where you can get ideas for multimedia projects. A great place to start is with your district technology coordinator. This person should be able to point you toward resources you can use. We do suggest that you join ISTE. They publish several journals that teachers find useful. *Learning and Leading with Technology* is one such journal that includes articles describing multimedia projects that teaches have used. ISTE also organizes a yearly conference, the NECC, that is attended by nearly 10,000 teachers, teacher educators, technology leaders, and technology companies. The conference offers a wealth of information and ideas dealing not only with multimedia but also other areas of technology and teaching and learning.

References

Gordon, D. T. (2000, June). *The digital classroom: How technology is changing the way we teach and learn.* Cambridge, MA: Harvard Education Letter.

International Reading Association and National Council of Teacher of English. (1996). *Standards for the English language arts.* Available: http://www.ncte.org/standards/standards.shtml [2001, Aug. 23].

International Society for Technology in Education. (2000). *National educational technology standards for students.* Eugene, OR: Author.

Recommended Reading

Brunner, C., & Tally, W. (1999). *The new media literacy handbook: An educator's guide to bringing new media into the classroom.* New York: Anchor.

Gibbs, J. (2000). *Tribes: A new way of learning and being together.* Winsor, CA: Source Systems LLC.

Talab, R. S. (May 2000). Copyright, plagiarism, and Internet-based research projects: Three "golden rules." *TechTrends, 44*(4), 7-9.

CHAPTER 3

Multimedia Projects in the Classroom

Chapter Guiding Questions

This chapter will help you answer the following questions:

- How can I use cooperative learning strategies to manage a classroom-based multimedia project?

- Where can I find multimedia production references suitable for students?

- What are my options for presenting and sharing students' multimedia projects?

As we mentioned in Chapter 1, one of the most compelling reasons for incorporating multimedia production projects into any classroom is the excitement these projects tend to generate among students. Learners of all ages have found digital multimedia production projects to be deeply satisfying educational experiences, and they enjoy sharing these projects with peers, other teachers, and parents.

Classrooms will vary widely in terms of available technological resources, but every teacher can make use of a set of relatively simple systematic technologies (methods of organization and management that have little to do with hardware) to establish and maintain a positive and productive environment for multimedia projects.

A Cooperative Learning Approach

Most teachers use a variety of instructional methods during the school year. These methods include lecture, independent study, problem-based learning, and discovery learning, to name but a few. These methods may be used individually or in combination with one another. Each instructional method has its own strengths and weaknesses, and many teachers develop a personal preference for a few methods that seem to work best for them based on their own personalities, the characteristics of their students, and the content they are teaching. An instructional method that seems to work particularly well for multimedia projects is cooperative learning.

Classroom multimedia projects are often approached as a cooperative learning opportunity for a very good reason: *Professional* multimedia production is a cooperative effort, demanding the skills and talents of a number of people working together for a common goal. Writers, managers, graphic artists, marketing specialists, researchers, and technicians are just a few of the many specialists required to create any multimedia product intended for mass distribution. See Figure 3.1 for a couple of examples.

A cooperative learning approach assumes that students will work in small groups (usually between four and six students per group). Students work in their groups as part of a team. Normally, the rewards (e.g. grades, evaluations, or credits) are shared equally by all members of the cooperative group. Members of the group work together with an "all for one and one for all" philosophy. As part of a production team, each group member makes best use of his or her strengths for the good of the group (e.g., some group members may be talented artists; others may be excellent managers).

Group members may be encouraged to develop skills by learning from other members of the team. For example, a student with a great deal of experience using photo manipulation software may be asked to share his or her knowledge with a group member who has not used this type of software before. Activities of this kind can be supported by including skill building into the project evaluation.

Classroom Management of Multimedia Projects

Managing a cooperative learning activity requires some special preparation on the teacher's part. Based on our experiences as classroom teachers and the research available on the subject of cooperative learning, we recommend the following five guidelines.

1. Set clear objectives for the groups.

Let them know what they need to accomplish. Generally, it is not enough to assign the task of creating something like a Web site without explicitly stating what the Web site should accomplish and a few production parameters as boundaries.

The following is an example of a well-written assignment (suitable for Grade 7 and up):

Work as a team to create a Web site that illustrates the life cycle of the monarch butterfly. The site should have no fewer than five pages and at least six photographs. The site should be designed for a monitor that has a 640 by 480 pixel (56 ppi) display and 256 color resolution. The finished project should include documentation that explains the site's design and the navigational strategy (or interface design) as well as thumbnail sketches or storyboard. The documentation should also include usability test results

---

Figure 3.1. How Many People Does It Take to Produce a Multimedia Product?

- The Living Book, *Arthur's Teacher Trouble,* lists over 60 people in its credits, including production managers, sound engineers, programmers, voice talent, and graphic artists.
- Over 150 people are listed in the acknowledgments and credits for Broderbund's *Where in the World is Carmen Sandiego?* Version 3.5.

(this may be a brief paper; be sure to include any artifacts that help to illustrate the production or usability testing process). Each member of the team must also submit a description of their personal experience with the project: what skills were developed and what challenges were faced (and how they were overcome).

For younger students it is probably most appropriate to greatly simplify or omit the documentation component of the assignment.

2. *Have individuals in each group take a specific role in the production.*

We have found it best to have team members take responsibility for a specific aspect of production. Articulating the various production roles helps students learn about types of jobs available in real-life multimedia production. Perhaps more important, this can be the starting point for conversations about teamwork and the strength of groups that have members with diverse skills and interests. Taking responsibility for a specific aspect of production should not limit a student's ability to participate in a variety of production aspects. For example, although one person may take primary responsibility for the artwork used in a presentation, other members of the team may contribute to the artistic effort.

3. *Plan opportunities for group members to talk about their experiences with students outside their own group.*

For example, if each group has a production manager, plan some time for all the production managers to get together and talk about what it means to manage a team.

4. *Monitor the groups carefully.*

Students may not know how to work together in a situation of this kind. The greatest danger in multimedia production activities is for one student to take over the entire project. Make sure the students continue to work together as a team.

5. ***Find ways to offer positive feedback to groups that are performing well.***

While monitoring the groups, look for opportunities to recognize and celebrate their developing abilities to resolve problems and successfully deal with challenges.

Media Production Role Call:
The Titles and Tasks of a Production Team

Any multimedia production may have a wide variety of roles for each team member to play. A few of the most critical roles include the following:

Production Manager: This person is responsible for the organization and timing of the production. It is the production manager's job to make sure that everyone knows what he or she should be doing and when they need to have specific tasks accomplished. The production manager is responsible for creating a production calendar (a set of due dates or "milestones" that keeps the production moving forward to the final due date). This is explained further in the description of how professional media is produced, later in this book. Examples of important production milestones include the following:

- Completing the first mock-up of the project
- Having all the text for the project typed and saved in digital form

Depending on the students' ages and abilities, the production manager may also be called on to resolve conflict within the group and to secure resources for the group.

Writer: This person is responsible for generating the text that may be necessary for the project. If a great deal of writing is required, it may be advisable to split this into two roles: writer for production (the person who handles text that is included in the multimedia presentation) and writer for documentation (the person who edits and coordinates the project write-up).

Checker: This person is responsible for making sure that any facts stated are correct. A second responsibility for the checker (among older students) is to ensure that any and all copyright questions are resolved before the project is completed.

Graphics Designer: This person is responsible for planning and producing all the graphic elements of the project. The graphics designer often does not create each graphic alone. More often, the graphics designer creates a vision of how the whole project should look in general (the types of images used, the colors that will dominate, the type style that will be used, etc.).

Interface Designer: This person is responsible for the interactive aspects of the project. The interface designer decides how content is divided (e.g., what content will go on what page of the Web site) and how the user will be able to access the content. The interface designer decides whether the navigation is linear or non-linear and where on the screen interactivity occurs (e.g., the placement of buttons, such as "next" or "back").

Tester: This person is responsible for making sure the project works the way it is intended to. The tester conducts a set of tests that informs the team how well they accomplished the goals of the assignment, how stable the product is, and what will need to be fixed in subsequent iterations of the multimedia project. The tester may arrange to have experts review the project; to have peers attempt to "break" the project (with digital multimedia, this usually means getting the computer to freeze or crash); and to have potential users try the product and report what they like and dislike about the product.

Talent: Any person or group that contributes to a multimedia production by performing (e.g., using their voices, their acting skills, posing for a photograph) is considered talent. These people are usually given credit for their work, but usually, there is not one person listed as "talent." It is usually the responsibility of the production manager to find and organize the talent.

Without including talent, we have listed six roles that are critical in multimedia production. Talent is not included as a critical role because it is possible to create a multimedia project that does not use human talent at all: It could be composed entirely of drawings or nonhuman sounds. If group size poses a potential problem (the ideal group size for younger students seems to be four; older students are often capable of working in larger groups), one person may take on more than one role. Some roles have greater responsibility at a specific point in time during the production process. For example, the tester's tasks are usually performed toward the end of the production, whereas the graphic designer may be busy throughout the entire production. If limiting the group size is important, we recommend combining the checker and the tester roles, and combining the interface designer and graphic designer roles.

Helping Students Learn Their Roles

Once everyone has taken responsibility for a specific role (either by assignment or by volunteering), they will need some opportunities to learn more about how best to perform their functions and how their role works with the other members of the production team. One strategy for teaching people about their roles is to hold brief, regular meetings with people who have the same role (in other words, all the production managers from all the groups would meet together; all the writers from all the groups would meet together, etc.). This strategy allows students to talk about their experiences with students who can directly empathize with them. Students may also share solutions to problems and gain a greater understanding of their responsibilities as manager, writer, designer, checker, or tester. This strategy of working with homogeneous groups has the added benefit of being particularly efficient: There is no need to have the same discussion about the role of the graphic designer multiple times.

Another strategy that is particularly efficient is to hold short workshops on specific aspects of the production process. Groups are invited to send one representative to attend the workshop; this person then becomes the group's resource for accomplishing the task the workshop covers. Workshops might be held for learning how to use specific hardware (such as flatbed scanners or digital cameras) or software (such as word processing, graphics manipulation, or authoring tools). Workshops might also be held for more general production tasks, such as creating storyboards or production calendars.

Allocating Resources

Multiple groups working simultaneously on multimedia projects may place a strain on classroom resources. With a little forethought and planning, everyone can have a satisfying experience without having to wait in line or argue about who has "dibbies" on the computer. In a classroom with limited computing tools, (say, one computer for the entire class, one digital camera, one flatbed scanner, etc.), we recommend creating a calendar that indicates when specific groups have access to specific resources. There are two possibilities for creating such a calendar:

1. Create a schedule that informs students when each group may access each of the resources; see Table 3.1 for an example.
2. Create a schedule that allows students to sign up for access to each of the resources (one might offer a sign-up option for blocks of time). Table 3.2 gives an example.

Table 3.1 A Schedule Designed to Inform Students When They May Access Resources

Group	Flatbed Scanner	Digital Camera	Authoring Software
Group 1	11:00 – 11:30	11:30 – 12:00	1:00 – 1:30
Group 2	11:30 – 12:00	1:00 – 1:30	11:00 – 11:30
Group 3	1:00 – 1:30	11:00 – 11:30	11:30 – 12:00

No system is perfect, and arguments will occur, but creating a schedule provides a structure that lets everyone know that they will have an opportunity to use the tools they need.

Table 3.2 A Schedule Designed to Allow Students to Sign Up for Resources

Resource	11:00 – 11:30	11:30 – 12:00	1:00 – 1:30
Flatbed Scanner			
Digital Camera			
Authoring Software			

Almost everyone will insist that they need the computer for great lengths of time. This is probably not the case if the project is carefully planned using "low media" to begin with. Even if access to computers is not a concern, it is a good idea to encourage students to create full mock-ups of their designs using paper and pencil (or to insist on it). This is also a sound instructional strategy, as Cornelia Brunner and William Tally (1999) point out in *The New Media Literacy Handbook:*

> As with any effort to master a new medium, students need time and opportunities to create multiple "drafts"—and have them warmly but critically reviewed—in order to be successful. In general, the "writing process" model of authorship is a good one to apply to any form of student creativity: Students should be given opportunities to brainstorm ideas important to them, "free-write" to explore the ideas, create several drafts in which meaning is both focused and elaborated, and receive feedback from peers and adults. (p. 5)

Beginning with low-media mock-ups and sketches is not just a good idea in a classroom setting, it is what real media producers do. For example, movies and animated short subjects are first created in "storyboard" format so that everyone working on the project has a strong sense of what the final product will look like before undertaking the effort and expense of filming. If classroom resources are limited, making sure that each group has a complete storyboard or mock-up (a preproduction procedure) before it begins production will help to ensure that everyone is making the best use of their computing time. See Figure 3.2 for a sample storyboard.

Rob McPherson and Julie Lippay teach at Franklin Elementary School in Pullman, Washington. They run an afterschool video club for fourth- and fifth-grade students.

Students work primarily on digital video projects produced using Avid Cinema and Apple's iMovie. Before any students may begin shooting or editing their videos, they must first create a script and a storyboard. The scripts and storyboards give students a road map to follow once they begin videotaping and editing.

Figure 3.2. A Sample Storyboard

An excerpt of a recent project script *(Lame Blond and Search for the GOLDENFRY,* a spoof on James Bond films), shows the level of detail the students reach in envisioning the finished product well before any multimedia production begins:

Scene 6

(The trip to America by rowboat)

Funny Money: Lame Blond, you and your partner must make the trip to America. You can choose any kind of transportation you want.

Lame Blond: I have just the thing. (Walking to the beach.)

Lame Blond: You're a good swimmer, right, Natalie?

Natalie: I guess so . . . why?

Lame Blond: Well, why don't we just swim to America? It would save us money, and it's only a short trip.

Natalie: Okay.

Lame Blond: But before we get going, I have to go back to my house to get my water wings.

(Lame Blond leaves and then comes back with his water wings.)

Lame Blond and Natalie: Good-bye, Funny Money.

(They swim away; a map is shown with little lines showing movement.)

Similar mock-up procedures (written descriptions and storyboards) can be used for interactive multimedia production as well. In the case of interactive media, some description of the interactivity must be created prior to production. Professionals often create a "navigation map" showing the relationships among each of the screens (HyperStudio "cards," PowerPoint "slides," and HTML "pages"). One of the simplest methods of creating a navigation map is to use Post-it notes and a piece of butcher paper, placing one Post-it note for each screen on the butcher paper and drawing lines indicating how individual screens connect to each other (for example, every screen might connect directly to a home screen).

Media Production References

We recommend establishing a small classroom library on the subject of multimedia production. This library can provide both information about how to accomplish production tasks and examples of the sketches and storyboards used by professional media producers to create popular movies, television shows, cartoons, and software. Two of the easiest things to obtain are sample storyboards and preproduction sketches.

Samples of these storyboards are available in book form and are often found on DVD versions of films. Books on "the making of" and "the art of" movies and movie studios are currently quite popular, and it may be worth investing in a small library of these titles to share with students. Books that contain preliminary sketches, mock-ups, and storyboards include the following:

- *The Art of Walt Disney: From Mickey Mouse to the Magic Kingdoms* by Christopher Finch (1995).

- *The Art of Return of the Jedi: Star Wars:* Including the Complete Script of the Film (The Art of Star Wars Series, No. 6) by Lawrence Kasdan and George Lucas. (1997).

Many famous movies publish their shooting scripts (the scripts used on the movie set). We found a wide variety of these scripts by searching amazon.com's book section, using the phrase, "shooting script." They are usually reasonably priced (under $20), and the selection is wide enough to appeal to many different age groups. A few shooting scripts make excellent references for young writers. Even for students who are not working on creating a movie, shooting scripts are excellent examples of using the written word to communicate the storyteller's vision to the artists who give that vision form.

Many DVD (digital video disk) editions of popular movies include pre-production artwork and storyboards. For example, the DVD versions of *Ghostbusters* (Reitman, 1984), the Beatles' *Yellow Submarine* (Dunning, 1968), and *X-Men* (Singer, 2000) include the storyboards and sketches used to make the films (more recent films, such as *X-Men,* also contain "animatic" sequences: a new type of animated storyboard).

At present, there are few really good books on the subject of creating multimedia projects that are appropriate for K-12 settings. These two seem to work reasonably well:

- *Interactivity by Design: Creating and Communicating With New Media* by Ray Kristof and Amy Satran (1995).

- *Designing Multimedia: A Visual Guide to Multimedia and Online Graphic Design* by Lisa Lopuck (1996).

Presenting and Sharing Work

Often, the most satisfying aspects of making something is sharing it with others. However, traditional methods of classroom sharing by hanging pictures in the room, sending home artwork for the refrigerator, and creating bulletin boards that include student work will not do multimedia productions justice (although we have seen some really wonderful bulletin boards showcasing students' storyboards and written descriptions of the production process). To experience it fully, a digital multimedia piece needs to be viewed on a computer. Currently, there are two methods of disseminating digital multimedia work: posting it on the World Wide Web or distributing it via CD-ROM.

Choosing a Multimedia Production Tool

There are two common methods of creating multimedia productions in the classroom: using HTML (HyperText Markup Language) or using a visual basic analog tool.

HTML

Although it is possible to create HTML from scratch using a word processor and HTML tags, it is much easier to make use of an HTML editing tool that generates the tags while students work in a WYSIWYG (what you see is what you get) environment. One of the nicest aspects of producing multimedia projects for the Web is that files are converted to the smallest size possible; images have to be converted to JPEG, GIF, or PNG format, which truncate the file size (dozens of these can be saved on a single floppy disk), and HTML files (files that end in .html or .htm) are also very small (dozens of these can usually fit on a floppy disk as well). Web work can be posted on a public Web server for the world to see, or can be saved onto a disk or local hard drive for more selective viewing.

The problem with multimedia work using just HTML is that HTML is deliberately limiting (in this way, files remain small and viewable on a variety of computers and operating systems). HTML does not allow students to easily place images wherever they would like them on the screen, nor does it allow for the easy creation of sophisticated user interfaces; one is pretty much limited to the traditional methods of Web surfing using hyperlinks. Also, it is difficult to get sound and video to work reliably using HTML (it is possible, but not easy). To easily create a versatile multimedia environment, one must make use of authoring tools more sophisticated than HTML editors.

Authoring Tools Based on Visual Basic

One of the easiest multimedia authoring tools (and often the most readily available in elementary school settings) is HyperStudio. There are other similar tools that vary in the degree to which they are easily mastered—generally, the more difficult the authoring tool is to learn, the more it is capable of doing (see Figure 3.3). Our list of the most popular authoring tools, in order of easiest to use to the most difficult, includes HyperStudio, ToolBook (works on PC platform only), HyperCard (works on Macintosh platform only), Authorware, and Director. All of these tools have one thing in common; they are derived from the visual basic programming language (the digerati refer to them as "VB analogs"), which allows more sophisticated users to go beyond the WYSIWYG aspect of the tool in to program it very specifically (in each case, using a programming language that looks a great deal like visual basic). The program PowerPoint is also a multimedia production tool, and the latest versions allow for the creation of more sophisticated interfaces, but PowerPoint is different from the others mentioned in that it is not derived from visual basic and is therefore not as flexible in terms of making specific modifications.

Posting Work to the World Wide Web

HTML work, whether created on a word processor using tags or created using HTML editing software, can be viewed via the World Wide Web as soon as it is transferred to a server directory. That is to say, the files are uploaded to a directory that is

---

Figure 3.3. Getting "Geeky" with HTML

Learning how to write and edit HTML tags is surprisingly easy. One of the best books we have seen on this subject is Elizabeth Castro's (1998) *Visual Quickstart Guide: HTML for the World Wide Web*. The author explains in easy-to-understand language how HTML tags work and provides a variety of examples. It is both a good instructional text and a good reference book.

We also recommend getting familiar with at least two HTML editors (often called Web editors). An HTML editor is a piece of software that works almost exactly like a word processor. Instead of preparing a document for printing, an HTML editor prepares a document for posting to the World Wide Web. Claris Homepage is one of the simplest editors to use; Adobe PageMill is another easy one. In terms of price, Netscape Composer cannot be beat: It is free to download (www.netscape.com—download the full Netscape Communicator package).

For more advanced HTML editing, software that has a steep learning curve may be more appropriate. Current industry favorites include Macromedia Dreamweaver, Microsoft Frontpage, and Adobe GoLive.

---

accessible through any networked computer. HTML is the native language of the Web and is the easiest type of file for a browser to decode and display.

Authoring tools often have the ability to export work in such a way that the work can be posted to the World Wide Web. This is sometimes referred to as *shocking* a file, because of the shockwave process created by Macromedia that allows Director files to be viewed on the Web. A file is shocked when it is saved (or exported) in such a way that it can be embedded into an HTML file—the best metaphor we have heard for this is that the shocked file "rents space" from the HTML file. To view a shocked file, a browser often needs to have a specific plug-in (a little extra bit of software) installed into it. This is usually quite easy to do if the browser is running on a computer that is connected to the Internet. HyperStudio, Director, and PowerPoint files are particularly easy to shock.

Many school districts have their own Web servers (computers dedicated to the task of posting information to the World Wide Web), and members of the district are usually encouraged to post information to the Web through allocated space on the district's server. If one is accessing the Internet through an independent Internet service provider (ISP), there is often an allocation of space on the ISP's Web server set aside for each paid account. It is also possible to purchase an allocation of Web space from private organizations that will even allow one to create a specific domain name (e.g., mrsolivesclass.org or scienceexperiments.org).

Burning Issues: Creating CD-ROMs

Creating a CD-ROM is referred to as *burning* because the process includes a tiny laser etching grooves into the plastic disk's surface (there is no exposure to laser light; it all takes place inside the CD-ROM burning unit). CD-ROM burning units are relatively inexpensive (around $250 for an external unit that plugs into the computer). The CD's can be purchased in quantity for less than 60¢ apiece (lots of 10 are often about $1 apiece, and even when sold individually, CDs are rarely more than $2.50 apiece).

Any files may be burned onto a CD-ROM, which is essentially a really big floppy disk that usually can only be written on once (some CD-ROMs can be rewritten). CDs are made entirely of plastic and are therefore less susceptible to damage from magnetism than other computer storage media, and CDs have an anticipated shelf life of over 80 years.

When creating a CD-ROM version of class projects, make sure that the files burned onto the CD include some method of displaying the project. For example, if the project is created in HTML, make sure browser software is included on the CD-ROM. If the project is one or more PowerPoint or HyperStudio files, make sure the appropriate "player" software is included on the CD-ROM. Player software is a small version of the authoring tool that allows a person to play a file without being able to change the file in any way (PowerPoint and HyperStudio player software is available free of charge). Another thing to consider is whether to create a CD-ROM that can be read by a Macintosh, a PC, or both (which is called a hybrid CD-ROM). CD-ROM-burning software usually offers a choice of these three options.

Creating CD-ROM versions of class projects allows students to walk away with something tangible (and kind of nifty! We still get a kick out of making our very own CDs). CD-ROMs can hold a tremendous amount of information; often, an entire class of group projects will fit onto one CD. Saving projects onto CD-ROMs also allows for some creative packaging, because the CDs require some type of storage (a paper sleeve or a plastic jewel box) that can accommodate artwork.

Credit Where Credit Is Due

Copyright issues are a little different when creating multimedia projects than they are for classroom teaching. If a project is to be posted to the World Wide Web or distributed via CD-ROM, formal copyright restrictions come into play. It is worth checking into the current copyright laws carefully. We recommend checking with the American Library Association or AECT; both organizations make it a point to keep up with copyright issues as they pertain to multimedia and classroom settings.

Basically, it is important not to use borrowed artwork, photographs, or software without receiving express permission from the owners of the work. (Just because a picture of Superman is visible on the World Wide Web does not mean that it is not free for anyone to copy and use.) Whenever artwork, photographs, or software are used with permission, it is appropriate to indicate the original owner in some way.

Something like "copyright DC comics: used with permission" should appear near any borrowed work.

Last But Not Least, Safety First

It is probably not news, but it is important to mention that safety is an issue whenever multimedia work includes the public display of names or photographs of students. We do not advocate placing the images and names of individuals on a publicly accessible Web page or a widely distributed CD-ROM because this information potentially can be used in a harmful manner. This is of course a matter of personal discretion, parental permission, and school policy. We recommend caution and careful consideration before publicly posting or distributing media that contains information about students.

Summary

Incorporating multimedia production projects into the classroom can generate a great deal of excitement. Classrooms will vary in terms of available media production resources, but every teacher can make best use of the resources available through careful planning. A cooperative learning approach to instruction is a popular method of managing multimedia production in the classroom, in part because this approach reflects how most professional multimedia producers function. Members of cooperative learning groups can take responsibility for specific production roles to facilitate and enrich the process. Teachers can hold small in-class workshops based on specific roles or specific production tasks, allowing students to interact with others outside of their assigned group.

No matter how well equipped a classroom is, it is necessary to manage resources so that all groups have an equal opportunity to use all materials. Emphasizing the creation of mock-ups, storyboards, and thumbnail sketches in the early stages of production helps to ensure that more sophisticated (and often more limited) resources are used to their best advantage. A small library of preproduction materials from easily recognized films, television, and cartoons helps illustrate the importance of thumbnails and storyboards.

Decisions must be made in advance about how digital multimedia will be produced and distributed. Two of the most elemental decisions are whether to create World-Wide-Web-based (HTML) files or files that are created using an authoring tool (usually, some analog of the visual basic programming language). These decisions will affect how the projects are distributed. Two particularly popular distribution options are to post to the World Wide Web or to create CD-ROMs.

Multimedia projects that are distributed beyond the classroom must address the issue of copyright. Copyright law protects those who create media. Permissions to use copyrighted work must be obtained, and credit should be given whenever a copyrighted work is incorporated into a multimedia project. Another legal and ethical consideration is that of safety if students' faces and names are used in a distributed multimedia production. Care must be taken to avoid putting any student at risk through public exposure.

Frequently Asked Questions About Multimedia Projects in the Classroom

Question: Does the fair-use policy of use of copyrighted material extend to classroom multimedia projects?

Answer: The fair-use policy that allows teachers to use such things as videotapes of broadcasts, book chapters, and copies of pictures in their classroom extends to multimedia projects as long as the projects are not made public (for example, through posting to the World Wide Web). The problem with digital multimedia is that it is easy to copy and distribute far beyond the classroom; any potential copyright infringements must be very carefully considered.

Question: Is there some way to post a public Web site with students' photographs that avoids putting them at risk?

Answer: One possibility is to alter the pictures using digital imaging software (the industry standard is Adobe's Photoshop). Using this type of software, photographic images can be made to look more like paintings or sketches, making students less recognizable. For the sake of safety, always avoid putting any child's picture and name together, even if the picture is altered.

Question: Where can I find out more about how other teachers incorporate multimedia projects into their classrooms?

Answer: Joining organizations such as ISTE entitles you to free subscriptions to journals such as *Learning and Leading With Technology.* Also, there are a variety of local, regional, national, and international conferences held each year on the subject of incorporating new technologies into the K-12 classroom: NECC is probably the largest of these held in the United States. More information about ISTE and NECC is available at: www.iste.org.

References

Castro, E. (1998). *Visual quickstart guide: HTML 4 for the World Wide Web.* Berkeley, CA: Peachpit.

Dunning, G. (Dir.). (1968). *Yellow Submarine.* Los Angeles, CA: MGM.

Finch, C. (1995). *The art of Walt Disney: From Mickey Mouse to the magic kingdoms.* New York: Harry N. Abrams.

Kasdan, L., & Lucas, G. (1997). *The art of Return of the Jedi: Star Wars: Including the complete script of the film* (The art of Star Wars series, No. 6). New York: Del Rey.

Kristof, R., & Satran, A. (1995). *Interactivity by design: Creating and communicating with new media.* San Jose, CA: Adobe.

Living books: *Arthur's teacher trouble* [CD-ROM]. (1992).

Lopuck, L. (1996). *Designing multimedia: A visual guide to multimedia and online graphic design.* Berkeley, CA: Peachpit.

Reitman, I. (Dir.). (1984). *Ghostbusters.* Los Angeles, CA: Columbia Tri-Star.

Singer, B. (Dir.). (2000). *X-Men.* Los Angeles, CA: 20th Century Fox.

Where in the world is Carmen Sandiego? (Version 3.5). (1987)[CD-ROM]. Available: Torrance, CA: Broderbund.

Recommended Reading

Brunner, C., & Talley, W. (1999). *The new media literacy handbook: An educator's guide to bringing new media into the classroom.* New York: Anchor.

Cruickshank, D., Bainer, D., & Metcalf, K. (1999). *The act of teaching* (2nd ed.). New York: McGraw-Hill.

CHAPTER 4

Evaluating Multimedia Projects

Chapter Guiding Questions

This chapter will help you answer the following questions:

- How do I evaluate multimedia projects my students create?
- How do I give both group and individual grades for projects done in teams?
- How do I create a grading rubric for a multimedia project?

Levels of Evaluation: Product, Process, and Content

Multimedia projects can be evaluated by a variety of methods; we are sure that this idea does not come as a surprise. What may not be as apparent, however, are the specific elements of multimedia projects that need to be considered when they are being evaluated.

Multimedia projects are traditionally evaluated based on a variety of elements that make up three levels—product, process, and content. Multimedia projects can be evaluated using only one of these levels, a combination of two of them, or all three. The levels used to evaluate depend on the goal and objectives the teacher has set for the project. The three levels are explained in the discussion to follow.

Product Level

Evaluating a multimedia project on the product level is to evaluate it in its *final form*. Elements associated with the product level deal with how well the product works and meets its purpose for the intended audience. The elements include the navigation scheme, the layout of the media elements, the functionality of the media elements, and the usability of the project.

A variety of questions can be asked that help evaluate a multimedia project on the product level. For example,

- Does the navigation scheme allow the user to easily move throughout the multimedia project?
- Is the layout of the project consistent?
- Do the media elements work (that is, does the sound work, are the video clips viewable, etc.)?
- Can the intended audience use the project for its intended purpose?

Process Level

The process level deals with *how* the multimedia project was completed by the team. In evaluating at the process level, how well a group worked together is the key. Questions that can be asked are as follows:

- How well did the group function together?
- Did each team member complete his or her role (or did one person do most of the work)?
- What did the group learn? (What skills were developed or honed?)
- How well did the group work through difficult situations?
- How reflective was the group on how they worked together?

Content Level

Grading a multimedia project on the content level is to evaluate the *ideas, concepts, and thoughts* portrayed in the product. Questions like the following can be asked:

- How thorough and accurate is the content provided?
- How creative and original are the ideas?
- Does the information provided give evidence that the team understands the content?
- Do grammar or spelling errors exist?

Grading Teams Versus Individuals

Multimedia projects are typically designed and developed in teams because of the skills, time, and resources needed to complete them. The reality, however, is that students need to have individual grades as well. (Although this may not be our preference, it is the current reality of schools and grading.) How can teachers equitably evaluate teams and individuals? Honestly, it can be a tricky situation.

A difference needs to be made between evaluation and giving a grade. Evaluating a project does not indicate the same thing as giving a grade; an evaluation takes place before a grade is given. Giving an individual a grade for a particular multimedia project can be done in numerous ways; one typical way is by giving each member of a team the same grade, based on the evaluation of the multimedia project. This is not necessarily the best method.

We believe that when assigning students to multimedia project teams, teachers should make sure that individuals have specific roles that can be evaluated separately from the other team members. This will allow individuals to be evaluated on how they specifically contributed to a project. Ensuring that each student has a role can be done by using a cooperative learning approach, in which individual accountability and positive interdependence are crucial for success (see Chapter 3). This will also help to ensure that one individual does not take over completing the project without the other team members.

Multimedia Grading Rubrics

The process for grading multimedia projects can be simplified and made equitable by developing rubrics. A *rubric* is a set of standards that indicate criteria that need to be met to reach a certain level of achievement. Typically, a range is indicated for each criterion listed on a rubric, indicating that the criteria can be met at different levels. Figure 4.1 is an example of a grading rubric that focuses primarily on the product level.

Additional elements can be added to the rubric shown in Figure 4.1 to incorporate specific content objectives. Christine Olmstead, a sixth-grade teacher at Mariposa Elementary School in Brea, California, uses a rubric to evaluate both the content and product of a PowerPoint presentation project on Ancient Egypt she has her students develop. The goal of the project is for students, working in teams of three, to research an aspect of Ancient Egypt and create a PowerPoint presentation depicting the topic. The presentation is presented to the entire class once it is completed. The rubric (see Figure 4.2) is similar to the one depicted in Figure 4.1.

Summary

Multimedia projects include a variety of elements, which can make the evaluation of the projects difficult. To simplify the evaluation process, it is important to think of multimedia projects on three levels—product, process, and content. Each of these levels has its own set of elements that can be used to evaluate a project. Each multimedia project can be evaluated on one, two, or three of these levels, depending on the goal and objective(s) set by the teacher. Developing a rubric that includes criteria by which the project will be graded makes evaluation manageable and provides students with specifics on what is expected.

Figure 4.1. A Sample Grading Rubric for Multimedia Projects

Grading is based on a 100-point scale.

Completion of the tasks (all assigned elements)	80 points
All aspects of production working correctly	± 5 points
Thoroughness of usability test	± 5 points
Thoroughness of preproduction (script, storyboards)	± 5 points
Neatness, spelling, organization	± 5 points

Frequently Asked Questions About Evaluating Multimedia Projects

Question: Is it better to have students work in teams rather than individually when creating multimedia projects?

Answer: Having students work in teams solves a critical problem that many teachers face in the classroom—limited resources. If thirty students are working individually, there will be a strain put on the available resources. Teams consisting of four or five students will help alleviate the demand for resources and allow projects to be completed in a shorter time period. It is much easier to schedule six teams to use three classroom computers than it is to schedule thirty individuals. An additional benefit of having students work together is that it imitates how multimedia professionals work. Multimedia professionals create products in teams. They do so to share expertise and to save time. Students working in teams not only learn how to develop multimedia projects, they can also learn how to work cooperatively.

Figure 4.2. PowerPoint Evaluation

Students included three different topics in their project.

Needs improvement	Fair	Good	Excellent
3	5	8	10

Students had at least 10 slides.

Needs improvement	Fair	Good	Excellent
3	5	8	10

Students provided references or citations.

Needs improvement	Fair	Good	Excellent
3	5	8	10

Students' writing was in their own words.

Needs improvement	Fair	Good	Excellent
3	5	8	10

Complete sentences with correct punctuation, grammar, and spelling were used.

Needs improvement	Fair	Good	Excellent
3	5	8	10

The project flowed well from one slide to the next.

Needs improvement	Fair	Good	Excellent
3	5	8	10

Sound was used effectively.

Needs improvement	Fair	Good	Excellent
3	5	8	10

Overall project was interesting and easy to follow.

Needs improvement	Fair	Good	Excellent
3	5	8	10

TOTAL POINTS /100 =

5 CHAPTER

How Professional Multimedia Is Produced

··

Chapter Guiding Questions

This chapter will help you answer the following questions:

- What are the phases creating multimedia projects?

- What tasks do multimedia professionals do as they go through these phases?

- How do students go through the phases to create multimedia projects?

It is often said that multimedia projects are never finished, they are simply abandoned. This is not to say that multimedia professionals quit projects because they are frustrated. Rather, they typically stop a project because it becomes too time consuming. With multimedia projects, there are always some things that can be done to improve them. There comes a point when those creating them simply must stop and move on to other projects.

Although the task of designing and developing multimedia can be a time-consuming and complex process, it doesn't need to be overwhelming. To ensure that the process isn't overwhelming, multimedia professionals deliberately go through a set of project phases—design, production, and distribution. In this chapter, a description is given of how multimedia professionals conduct each phase. Explanations are provided in detail to help you learn how to successfully complete your own multimedia projects and teach your students how to do the same.

Phase One: Design

Step 1. Articulating the Vision of the Finished Multimedia Project

• Before multimedia professionals begin a multimedia project, a clear articulation of why the project is being produced is given. The following question is asked: What problem is the multimedia project meant to solve? There can be a variety of answers to this question. No matter what problem the project is meant to solve, it must be clearly identified at the beginning of the project.

• What are the goals and objectives of the project? All multimedia projects need to have clearly articulated goals and objectives. Multimedia professionals keep these in mind as they develop a project. The goals and objectives of a multimedia project influence how it is designed. Multimedia professionals make sure that they are aware of the goals and objectives before they begin the design process.

• Envision how the user will actually use the project. Multimedia producers, often with the help of their clients, describe a detailed scenario of the typical use of the finished product. They answer the following questions: When will the user have access to the product? Will the user need any special assistance in using the product? Will it be used by an individual or by groups? All of the possibilities of how a user or users will use the product are determined.

• Once the multimedia project is clearly articulated, multimedia professionals define and agree (normally with their client) to a set of production milestones. Production milestones are the important events that must be completed for the multimedia project to be finished successfully. These events are recorded on a production calendar. In setting up a production calendar, multimedia professionals start with the due date and go backward to the start date. It is good practice to require or agree to have the final product completed two days before it is actually due (this allows for the unexpected—technology failure, individuals getting sick during the production phase, and so forth—and still make the due date).

• The final stage before Phase Two (production) is to storyboard the project. A *storyboard* is a rough sketch on paper of how the final product will look (typically, plain white paper that represents the relative size of the final product is used—half a sheet of an 8" x 11" sheet of paper could represent one computer screen). The sketches should include representations of the media elements that will appear on different screens in the multimedia projects. For example, if a screen includes text, an image, and a sound clip, all of these elements should be sketched out, labeled, and placed where they would appear in the final product. The sketches should include the navigation. A storyboard helps to create a sense of how the different parts of the final product will fit together. Multimedia professionals don't begin developing their project on the computer until they have thoroughly gone through the design phase; it is easier to make changes on paper than it is on the computer (see Figure 5.1 for some of the reasoning).

Figure 5.1. "Fast, Cheap, or Good"

When thinking about multimedia projects, producers typically tell their clients that they can have only two of these: fast, cheap, or good. The clients must choose which two of the three fits their needs the most. For example, if a client needs a product to be developed in a very short amount of time and wants the quality to be high, the cost will be high because it will take a great deal of resources to finish it quickly. However, if the cost must be kept low and it still needs to be created in a short amount of time, then the product quality will suffer.

Phase Two: Production

Step 2. Gathering and Developing Media Elements

Once Phase One is completed, multimedia professionals begin putting a project together on the computer. The first step in this phase is gathering and developing the different media elements of the project. To determine the media elements, multimedia professionals look carefully through the storyboard and list all of the media elements that have been sketched out (that is, the text, audio, video, and images). Most likely, these elements will need to be created; however, some may already exist. The media elements that do not already exist are created (e.g., taking photographs, scanning images, recording audio and video, conducting research on the topic, writing text, and drawing illustrations). All images, audio, and video are put into a digital format (see Chapter 1 for a discussion of digital format). This is done in different ways depending on the media element. For example, if an image of a house is needed for the project, a photograph from a book could be used. The photograph would need to be scanned; scanning the image turns it into a digital format that now can be used by a computer. Digital media elements can be gathered from various locations and do not necessarily need to be created directly by the multimedia professionals. Media elements can be found on the Web (see Chapter 2 for Web sites) or purchased on CD-ROMs (multimedia professionals are careful to always cite where media elements are taken from). See Figure 5.2 for some tips from the professionals.

Step 3. Prototyping

After gathering all the necessary media elements, multimedia professionals begin putting the project together. The professionals do a variety of activities, such as developing the navigation scheme; importing images, audio, and video; choosing background colors; choosing text colors; and entering textual information. (See Figure 5.3 for some examples of software used by the professionals to put the elements

---

Figure 5.2. Tips and Tricks the Professionals Use

There are a variety of tips and tricks that professional multimedia producers use in developing their products. Here is a sampling of tips and tricks that we find useful and important.

Use Faces to Gain Attention: Human beings are naturally drawn to faces and images of faces (that is why most cereal boxes have faces of people or cartoon characters on the front and why most billboard advertisements include a face as a key element).

Design to the Lowest Common Denominator: Always design for a computer screen size of 640 by 480 (pixel width by pixel depth) and use the "Web Safe" color palette (216 colors that look correct on almost every monitor).

Text Size and Type: Use an easy-to-read type style for body text (Times and Times Roman are considered particularly readable), and use a type style that radically differs from the body text for headings (with Times and Times Roman, many people use Helvetica or Arial at a much larger size).

---

together.) Typically, a finished product goes through several development cycles called *prototypes*. The product is refined and improved with each cycle; therefore, a prototype is not the finished product. The purpose of a prototype is to allow others to see what the project will look like in a digital format (i.e., on the computer) and to determine how the project is progressing. Multimedia projects can go through numerous prototypes; however, due to time constraints, projects will generally have only one prototype before the final product.

Step 4. Usability Testing

Usability testing consists of allowing those who will use the product to see how well the product works. A typical usability test consists of a user or users interacting with the product—as a prototype and then the final product—in as real a context as is possible. The user(s) use the product for a specified amount of time and are asked to complete a series of tasks determined by the multimedia professionals. The tasks are based on the goals and objectives of the project. A typical usability test is conducted in the following manner by multimedia professionals: For example, let's say a multimedia project is being developed for sixth-grade students that will introduce them to different types of rocks. After a prototype of the product has been developed, two students are selected to use the product. The professionals will instruct the students to go through and use the product, giving them specific tasks they must complete or questions they must answer (such as, In what states would you find limestone? Or, Find the location in the project where you can see different pictures of rocks). As the students use the product, the multimedia professionals would note how the students used it, comments they made, bugs (errors) that came up, and how long it took them to do the different tasks (and if they could even accomplish

---

Figure 5.3. "Geek Speak": Software Tools that Professionals Use

Professional multimedia producers use a variety of software tools to help them produce multimedia projects. A sampling of different professional-quality software tools follows. The cost of these programs is not cheap (for instance, Adobe PhotoShop 6.0 is approximately $600). The good news is that most of the software tools are also sold at an educational price, which can often be half of the regular price! Additional good news is that the educational versions are almost always exactly like the professional versions (that is, they have the same functions and capabilities). The only stipulation that educational versions have is that the products created by using them cannot be sold or distributed commercially.

Another option for obtaining software tools to use in producing multimedia projects is to use freeware or shareware. Freeware and shareware are software that costs little or nothing to use. You can get freeware and shareware on the Web (it is a great place to start). The drawbacks to using freeware or shareware are that the quality of the software tools is not as high as the professional versions and the support and documentation available for using the software tools is often low or nonexistent.

- Graphic Manipulation: Tools that allow images to be created or altered
    Adobe PhotoShop
    Adobe Illustrator
    Macromedia Freehand
- Multimedia Authoring: Tools used to put media elements together to create a final interactive product (see Chapter 2 for a detailed description)
    Macromedia Director
    Macromedia Authorware
    Asymmetric Toolbook
- Sound Editing: Tools that allow for audio to be recorded and edited
    Macromedia SoundEdit16
- Video Editing: Tools that allow for video to be edited
    Adobe Premiere
    Apple Final Cut Pro
- HTML Editing: Tools that allow for the development of Web pages
    Macromedia Dreamweaver
    Microsoft FrontPage
    Claris Homepage
    Adobe GoLive
    Netscape Composer

---

the tasks). At the end of the session, the students would be asked for their reactions to the product. Reactions vary depending on the age and sophistication of your students; however, their comments might include that it was difficult to read the text because of the background colors used or that there were too many choices and they got lost in the product. It can be a humbling experience for multimedia professionals to have users critique their work. It is, however, a very important part of the design-and-development process of a multimedia project.

Step 5. Making Changes

The information collected in a usability test on a prototype will provide important information on how a product should be changed. With this information, multimedia professionals work on the prototype to improve it. After changes are made and the multimedia professionals test the product themselves, it is ready for Phase Three: Distribution. (Ideally, the product should go through another round of usability testing; however, time constraints may not make this possible. A second usability test would be conducted in the manner mentioned previously. The additional information gathered would be used to improve the product.)

Phase Three: Distribution

Step 6. Packaging and Distributing the Final Product

• Once the product is in its final form, decisions need to be made on how the product will be packaged and distributed. There are a variety of ways that this can happen; it really depends on where and how the product will be used. Is the product designed to be viewed on the Web? Is the product to be used solely in the classroom, or will students be allowed to take a copy home to use? Will students share the product with other students? The way the product is packaged and distributed will typically be determined by the client.

• Most multimedia professionals indicate to their clients that most multimedia products require a significant amount of storage space because of the media elements used; therefore, they will most likely not fit on a 3.5" floppy disk. The final products will need to be saved on a hard-drive or a Zip disk or burned onto a CD-ROM.

Summary

Producing successful multimedia projects can be a complex process; however, it is not an impossible one. Successful multimedia producers follow basics steps that are grouped into three phases—design, production, and distribution. It is important for the success of a multimedia project that the producer deliberately goes through each of these phases.

Frequently Asked Questions About
How Professional Multimedia Is Produced

Question: Is it necessary that I go through all of the phases listed in this chapter when creating a multimedia project?

Answer: Yes! The phases are designed to help you successfully complete multimedia projects. It is important to be true to the phases, especially if you are new to the process. Ignoring one of the phases could jeopardize the success of your project.

Question: Will my students have time to go through all of the phases in developing a multimedia project?

Answer: It definitely can be time-consuming having your students go through each of the phases. As mentioned, however, it is very important that all of the phases be completed. It may be necessary to modify how your students go through the steps. For example, you will most likely not have adequate time to have your students go through multiple rounds of usability testing.

Question: Many of the software tools listed in this chapter are expensive. Are there inexpensive options that will allow me to do the things my students and I will need to do?

Answer: Many of the software tools listed are available at reduced rates for teachers and students (you can get an "academic price"). Another place to look for less expensive software tools is on the Web at sites that offer shareware or freeware.

Recommended Reading

Brown, A. H., Green, T. D., & Zatz, D. (2000, May). Getting the most out of multimedia productions projects: A set of management guidelines. *Executive Update Online* [Online]. Available: http://www.gwsae.org/ExecutiveUpdate/2000/May/ElectronicIssue/index.htm [August 30, 2001].

Brunner, C., & Talley, W. (1999). *The new media literacy handbook: An educator's guide to bringing new media into the classroom.* New York: Anchor.

Elin, L. (2001). *Designing and developing multimedia: A practical guide for the producer, director, and writer.* Boston: Allyn & Bacon.

Kristof, R., & Satran, A. (1995). *Interactivity by design: Creating and communicating with new media.* San Jose, CA: Adobe.

Nieders, J. (1999). *Web design in a nutshell: A desktop quick reference.* Cambridge, MA: O'Reilly.

Nielsen, J. (1999). *Designing Web usability: The practice of simplicity.* Indianapolis, IN: New Riders.

Rada, R. (1995). *Interactive media.* New York: Springer Verlag.

White, R., Downs, T., & Adams, S. (2001). *How computers work: Millennium edition* (5th ed.). Indianapolis, IN: Que.

Winograd, T. (1996). *Bringing design to software.* Glenview, IL: Addison-Wesley.

Zettl, H. (2000). *Video basics.* Florence, KY: Wadsworth.

Appendix:
A History of Multimedia

Visionary and/or Date	Media Element	Event
Gutenberg and Caxton (1455)	Text	Invented the movable-type printing press
Babbage (1822)	Interactivity	Designed the difference machine, an early precursor to the microcomputer
Morse (1837)	Audio	Invented the telegraph receiver and transmitter
Daguerre (1839)	Still graphics	Invented the daguerreotype, photographs produced using a paper negative
Boole (1854)	Interactivity	Developed binary mathematical language of 0 and 1, the language all computers understand
1867	Text	Remington manual typewriter developed
Bell (1876)	Audio	Invented the telephone
Edison (1879)	Audio	Invented the phonograph
1888	Moving images	Sequential photography with sprockets manually pulled through a projector developed
1888	Audio	Mood music for film developed—musical scores sent along with films for live organ accompaniment
Hollerith (1890)	Interactivity	Developed tabulating machine for the United States government census using punch cards
1920	Audio	First commercial radio station, KDKA, went on the air in Pittsburgh

Visionary and/or Date	Media Element	Event
1925	Audio	AT&T's Bell lab allowed recording of whole symphonies
1927	Moving images	The first commercial talking film produced (*The Jazz Singer*) using optical sound recording
Disney (1928)	Moving images and still graphics	Produced *Steamboat Willie*, first cartoon with fully synchronized soundtrack
Zuse (1931)	Interactivity	Developed the first calculator
1932	Storage	Magnetic tape developed; BASF introduced magnetic tape recording
Antanasoff (1939)	Interactivity	Developed a prototype of the ABC computer—the first automated digital computer
1940	Moving images	First color TV program broadcast
1948	Interactivity	The transistor was developed—more reliable and cheaper to run than vacuum tubes
1951	Storage	UNIVAC developed—computer using magnetic tape for buffer memory
1952	Interactivity	IBM 701 developed: First electronic stored computer, which used vacuum tubes, RAM, and punch cards and was the size of a piano
1956	Audio	First network broadcast using videotape was aired
1958	Interactivity	CRAY computer developed; CDC 1604 built for Control Data Corporation—the first fully transistorized supercomputer
1959	Interactivity	IBM introduced the second generation of computers, which used transistors instead of vacuum tubes
1960	Storage	Removable disks developed
1963	Still graphics	CAD (Computer Aided Design) developed; Sketchpad used the first light pen
1963	Video	First home video tape recording introduced
1963	Audio	Phillips created first compact audio cassette
Nelson (1965)	Interactivity	Developed Xanadu hypertext project
1970	Interactivity	Fourth-generation computer created by IBM, which used chips to reduce the size and cost
1972	Moving images	Phillips created laserdisc playback-only deck
1972	Interactivity	PONG—first commercial video game appeared on the market

Visionary and/or Date	Media Element	Event
Kahn and Cerf (1973)	Internet	Ideas for the structure of the Internet outlined
Gates (1975)		Microsoft founded
1975	Moving images	Sony Betamax VCR introduced
1976	Moving images	JVC introduced VHS format
Jobs and Wozniak (1977)		Founded Apple Computers
1977	Internet	E-mail provided to 100 researchers
1979	Interactivity	VisiCalc—the first spreadsheet—and Wordstar—the first word-processing package—introduced
1979	Audio	Sony Walkman introduced
1979	Internet	Online services began, with CompuServe and The Source
1980	Moving images	Sony introduced the consumer camcorder
1981	Interactivity	MS-DOS operating system, the precursor to Windows, developed by Microsoft
1982	Still graphics	The first computer-generated graphics used in Disney's *Tron*
1982	Audio	First digital audio compact disc introduced
1983	Audio	Musical instrument digital interface (MIDI) introduced
1983	Internet	TCP/IP Protocol first used by the Internet
1984	Interactivity	Apple Computers introduced the Macintosh; the first computer using a mouse-driven graphical user interface (GUI)
1984	Storage	3.5″ floppy diskette introduced
1985	Storage	CD-ROMS evolved from music CDs
1987	Interactivity	HyperCard, introduced by Apple—authoring system allowing for interactive multimedia to be developed
1988	Still graphics	3-D graphics—3-D graphical super-computers introduced
1989	Interactivity	Fully functional, battery-powered notebook computer introduced
1989	Interactivity	SimCity simulation released by Maxis Software—new genre of software developed
1990	Interactivity	IBM, Tandy, and AT&T announced the hardware specifications for multimedia platform computers

Visionary and/or Date	Media Element	Event
1990	Internet	World Wide Web—HTML (HyperText Markup Language) developed
Andreessen (1993)	Internet	Mosaic—precursor to Netscape and Internet browsers—developed
1995	Storage	CD-ROM recorders available for microcomputers
1996	Still graphics	Digital cameras available

Glossary

....

Analog: Refers to a method of representing as series of continuously varying physical quantities.

Authoring tool: Refers to any software that coordinates a computer-based multimedia presentation. HyperStudio is an authoring tool; a Web editor is an authoring tool.

Browser: Software that interprets HTML, generally used to display Web pages on a computer.

CD-ROM (Compact disk–read-only memory): A high-capacity, digital information storage medium.

Cooperative learning: An instructional strategy requiring students to work in small groups addressing a topic or project. Members of the group typically assume specific roles and take equal responsibility for the final outcome of the activity.

Curriculum: A prescribed course of study.

Digital: A method of representing information as a series of bits that represent *on* or *off* states.

DVD (digital video disk): Similar to CD-ROM, DVD is a high-capacity, digital storage medium currently used most often for storing and playing feature-length movies.

Geek: Throughout this book, this term is used reverentially to refer to any person who is comfortable and competent with computing tools.

GIF (graphic interchange format): A compact digital image file format that can be viewed using a browser.

Grading rubric: A set of evaluation criteria applied to an assignment.

HTML (HyperText Markup Language): A library of commands that format text, graphics, and sound into documents that can be seen in a browser.

HyperStudio: A multimedia authoring tool marketed by Knowledge Adventure, particularly popular in elementary and middle school settings.

Internet: The worldwide network of all computers using the "transfer control protocol/ Internet protocol" (TCP/IP), generally considered the combination of all computer-based communications activity (e.g., e-mail, World Wide Web).

ISTE: International Society for Technology in Education.

JPEG (joint photographers expert group): A compact digital image file format that can be viewed using a browser.

Media: The plural form of medium; any type of visual or aural communication.

Multimedia: Any method of transmitting information using more than one medium.

PNG (portable network graphic): A compact digital image file format that can be viewed using a browser.

PowerPoint: A multimedia authoring tool developed by Microsoft, used primarily for making projected presentations.

Prototype: A model of the final product. Prototypes range from simple sketches to fully operational models.

Script: A text-only version of a multimedia project.

Storyboard: A set of sketches that illustrates the sequence of events in a multimedia project.

Usability testing: A method of evaluating the users' ability to navigate and comprehend a multimedia project.

Visual basic: A programming environment that offers graphic depiction of interactive events. The most common events include creating a button or animation.

Web editor: Software that facilitates the creation of HTML files.

World Wide Web: The collection of publicly available HTML files that any person with a computer connected to the Internet and browser software may view.

WYSIWYG (what you see is what you get): An interface design term referring to a direct correlation between the user's intention and the action depicted on the screen.

Index

The Corwin Press logo—a raven striding across an open book—represents the happy union of courage and learning. We are a professional-level publisher of books and journals for K–12 educators, and we are committed to creating and providing resources that embody these qualities. Corwin's motto is "Success for All Learners."